MW00769873

pocket posh
· · · · · · · · · ·
take care

Inspired Activities
for **Tranquility**

pocket posh

· · · · · · · · · ·

take care

Inspired Activities
for **Tranquility**

Andrews McMeel
PUBLISHING®

We all need some time to focus on ourselves. It's easy to become overwhelmed—by work, by home responsibilities, by the news of the day. It's important to step away, relax, and recenter. *Take Care: Inspired Activities for Tranquility* invites you to practice small moments of self-care through mindful activities, inspirational words, and thought-provoking journal prompts.

Take some time for yourself.

. . . take care.

"The great benefit of slowing down is reclaiming the time and tranquility to make meaningful connections— with people, with culture, with work, with nature, with our own bodies and minds."

—Carl Honoré

```
R  T  R  O  U  T  B  S  M  E  L  T
D  O  J  P  X  S  Z  E  W  X  O  C
I  M  M  J  E  S  H  A  R  Z  L  I
R  I  Z  E  N  R  S  A  Z  L  L  L
D  L  Y  E  C  R  C  X  R  K  I  F
A  E  H  J  A  H  Y  H  Z  K  P  N
M  T  X  W  V  I  E  N  N  A  O  O
A  L  I  S  B  O  N  F  J  X  P  C
```

find and circle

Seven European capitals	⊘○○○○○○
Four five-letter fish	○○○○
Two eight-letter words	○○
Chief cook	○
1,760 yards	○

3

lion's breath

As you do this exercise, imagine that you're a lion. Let all of your breath out with a big, open mouth.

STEP 1: Sit comfortably on the floor or in a chair.

. . . .

STEP 2: Breathe in through your nose. Fill your belly all the way with air.

. . . .

STEP 3: When you can't breathe in anymore, open your mouth as wide as you can. Breathe out with a "HA" sound.

. . . .

STEP 4: Repeat several times.

. . . .

DOT TO DOT

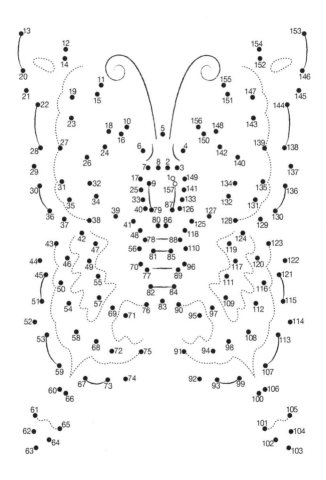

5

journal prompt

Sit quietly for a few minutes, breathing and listening to your body before you begin.

What is one long-term goal you wish to work toward?
. . . .

Write a letter to your future self.
. . . .

Write about how you would spend a day doing things that make you feel excited, happy, engaged, or fulfilled. Include everything you would do on this day, from the time you wake up until you head to bed at night.
. . . .

"Whatever's not full makes noise.
Whatever is full is quiet."

—*Buddha*

BUBBLEBATH By Anna Gundlach

ACROSS

1. Belonged to a cast
6. Communcation system for Deaf communities: Abbr.
9. The things over there
10. Kathy who was in "Misery"
12. Dalai Lama's homeland
13. French river that passes through Lyon
14. Vote of dissent
15. "Selma" director DuVernay
17. Sports org, for Tiger Woods
18. French diarist Anais
19. Chef's protection
20. Relaxing soaks, as visualized by this puzzle
24. Perlman of "Cheers"
25. Turn on the waterworks
26. Winter hours in NJ
27. "Alias" initials
28. Small baking qty.
31. Personal teacher
33. Secret stockpile
35. Pay for, as dinner
36. Mac & cheese pasta shape
37. Goof up
38. Eye maladies

DOWN

1. Business mail abbr.
2. Fad "Pet" whose seeds are a superfood
3. Country singer Keith with twenty #1 hits
4. Direction opposite WNW
5. Small part of the big picture
6. Noise of delight you might make when you get into a hot tub
7. "That's enough!"
8. TV show's duration
10. Undergarment with hooks
11. Airplane reservations
16. T-shirt style
18. Trail Blazers' org.
19. Asian Pacific American Heritage Month
20. Football's Favre
21. "I guess that sounds true . . . "
22. Fully recovered
23. Alternative to Invisalign
27. Marina Abramovic's work, e.g.
28. Frozen dessert franchise
29. Clog or mule
30. Rows in a church
32. Rower's propeller
34. Genre modifier before rock and country

"Time you enjoy wasting is not wasted time."

—*Marthe Troly-Curtin*

find and circle

Nine words that begin and end with "R"   ⊘○○○○○○○○

Four drinking vessels   ○○○○

A 12-letter word   ○

Goddess of love and beauty   ○

Fruit with yellowish skin and pinkish pulp   ○

write a letter

We would never talk to our best friend in the same critical way we sometimes talk to ourselves. As a reminder to be kind, write a letter to yourself as if your best friend were writing it to you. What advice and words of comfort would they write?

. . . .

. . . .

. . . .

. . . .

. . . .

. . . .

. . . .

. . . .

. . . .

"There are always
flowers for those who
want to see them."

—*Henri Matisse*

find and circle

Six words that contain "OO" (four-letter min.)	⊘○○○○○
Six five-letter styles of dance	○○○○○○
Two opposing sides in a sporting event	○○
Two Microsoft Office programs	○○
Two things to drink coffee from	○○

18

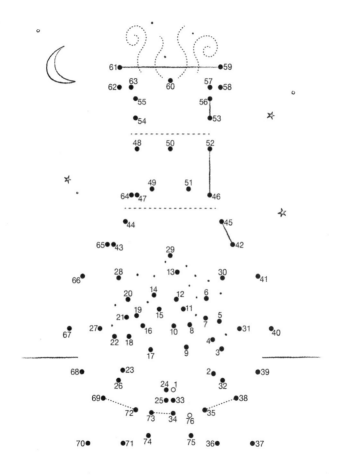

19

5-4-3-2-1 mindfulness break

Write five things you can SEE in the room.

. . . .

Write four things you can FEEL.

. . . .

Write three things you can HEAR.

. . . .

Write two things you can SMELL right now.

. . . .

Write one thing you can TASTE.

. . . .

"I slept and dreamt that life was joy. I awoke and saw that life was service. I acted and behold, service was joy."

—*Rabindranath Tagore*

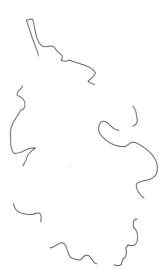

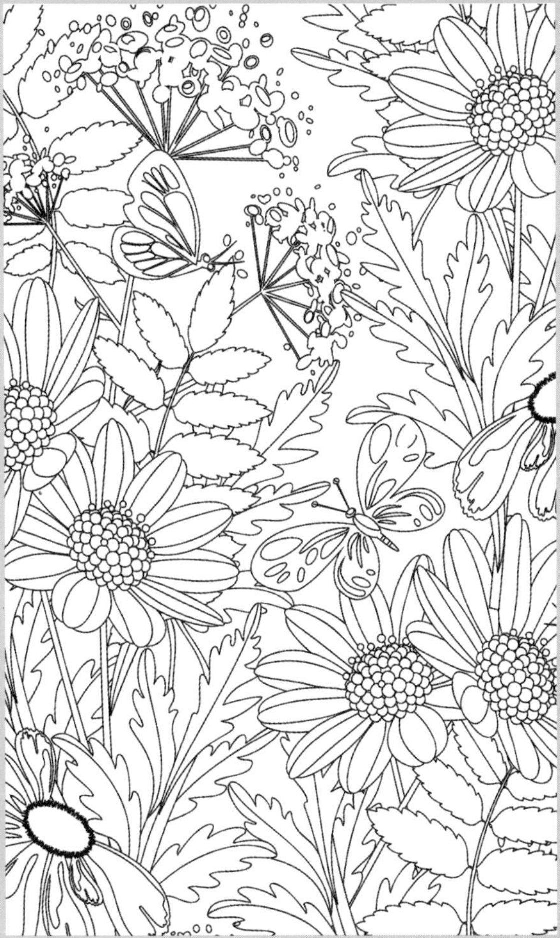

JOY By Anna Gundlach

ACROSS

1. Altar vow
4. Preparation for action
8. Email that hopefully will be automatically deleted
9. City that surrounds the Vatican
10. Part of a princess costume
11. Trade show, for short
12. Mindful question asked by this puzzle's dedicatee, with 26-Across
14. Forget to carry the one, e.g.
15. "Curiously Strong" breath mint
19. Best-selling author and organization consultant, with 22-Across
22. See 19-Across
23. Microfiber cleaning towel
25. It's all around you
26. See 12-Across
29. Vegan food staple
32. Rushed toward
33. Emanation from the compost bin
34. Bit of coffee sediment
35. Perimeter
36. Put on an elbow patch, maybe

DOWN

1. Bitter brews
2. Object thrown at bars
3. Nebraska metropolis
4. "Abracadabra!"
5. Salmon for bagels
6. Sound booster at a music venue
7. "The Matrix" role for Keanu
8. ___ Club (environmental preservation group)
10. Sacred scripture
12. They usually win in blue states, informally
13. Sort
16. In for the long haul on a pub crawl, say
17. Chowderhead
18. Fish who found Nemo
20. "No doubt about it"
21. Japanese royal: Abbr.
24. Football units
27. Hard to come by
28. Had no doubt about
29. Pedicured part
30. Abnormal
31. Common San Francisco weather forecast

"Now and then it's good
to pause in our pursuit
of happiness and just
be happy."

—*Guillaume Apollinaire*

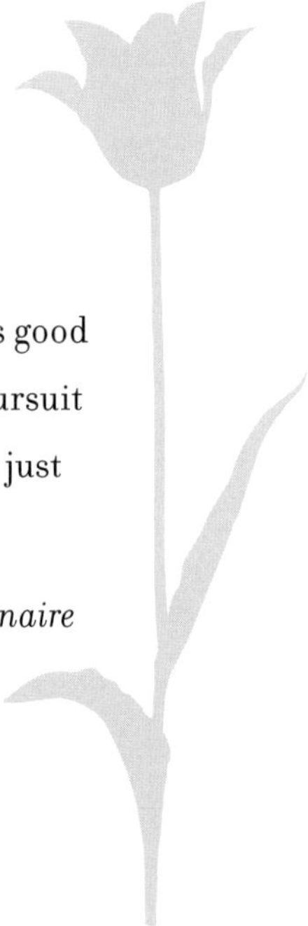

C L I B Y A Y C K Z A Z
A U J K S Z P L H I X T
L X B Z O C I A S I I Y
G V Y A M M A S N U N N
E C R E A M U N R A I A
R O W L L R K F A O M Z
I T U N I S I A C D X A
A J A M A I C A Y Z A J

find and circle

Ten countries ending in "A"	⊘○○○○○○○○○
Two dairy products	○○
Orange or apple, for example	○
Nickel or dime, for example	○
Bird of prey with a three-letter name	○

29

pressure point relaxation

There are pressure points on the bottoms of your feet that can help relieve stress and relax your muscles. Roll a golf ball under the entire sole of your foot using various pressures for maximum benefit.

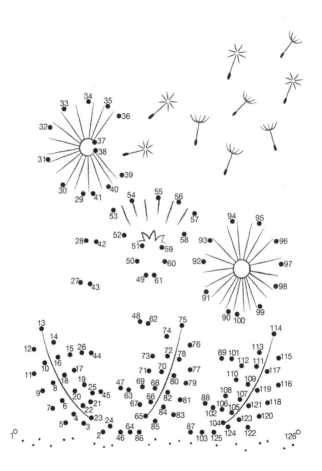

31

journaling prompt

Sit quietly for a few minutes, breathing and listening to your body before you begin.

How do I find fulfillment?

. . . .

What are three things that I love about myself?

. . . .

What are three unhealthy habits I need to cut out of my life?

. . . .

"Life itself is the most wonderful fairy tale."

—*Hans Christian Andersen*

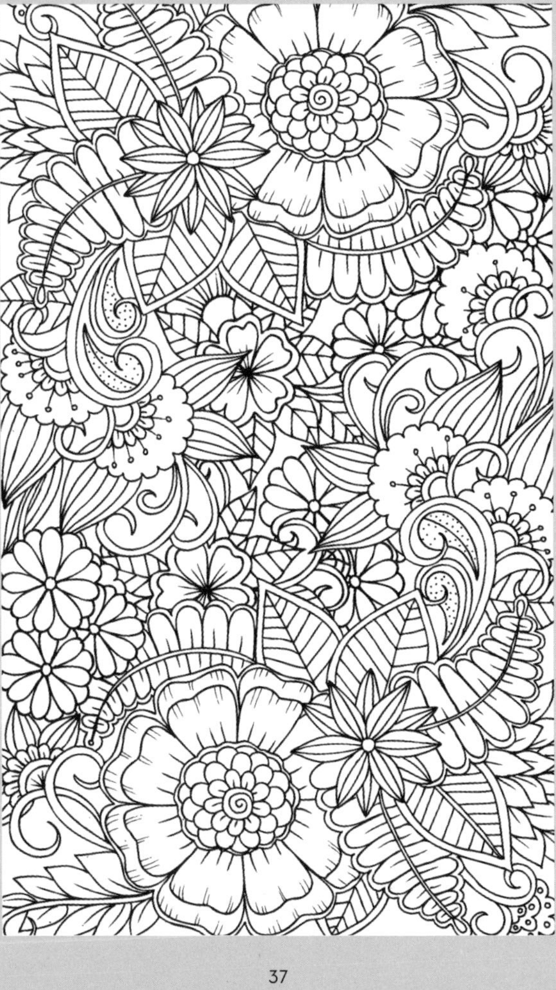

REST & RELAXATION By Anna Gundlach

ACROSS

1. Make a donation
5. Dressy-casual polo brand
9. Traveller's stop
10. Theatrical digression
11. "Wicked Games" singer Chris
12. Hauled off to jail
13. British luxury car
15. Lilly of pharmaceuticals
16. Batteries in some mice
17. 1958 hit covered by Michael Jackson in 1972
23. Cease
24. Guy on a fiver
25. Enthusiastic endorsement
29. Grocery store division
30. Occupy, as a dinner table
31. Stand-in
32. Looks to be
33. Get wind of
34. Chances at the casino

DOWN

1. Leave the band to write your own music
2. Writing with a bias?
3. Wiener schnitzel meat
4. ___ Club (fraternal group)
5. Parental veto, after "because"
6. Metal that makes up 97.5% of a penny
7. Comics dog with a huge tongue
8. Badger's lair
9. Person looking to fill a job opening
10. Like an enthusiastic crowd
14. Relaxing time off . . . and a hint to this puzzle's theme
18. Bulletproof vest material
19. "___ a vacation after that week!"
20. Prepared a fishhook
21. Letter-shaped construction pieces
22. Salamanders in a witch's brew
25. Bat mitzvah or baptism
26. In international waters, e.g.
27. Exxon, outside of the USA
28. Competed (for)
29. Something a Juul doesn't make

"Keep smiling
because life is a
beautiful thing,
and there's so
much to smile
about."

—*Marilyn Monroe*

```
F T E L E V I S I O N C
D I R I N G O J O H N A
O B S Z G E O R G E Y T
G I T H A M S T E R A R
Z R R M A S K Y E L W A
B D A V Z N A U A U B D
Z Z I X I R L E Z A U I
S X N P G B T K X P S O
```

find and circle

Five animals often kept as pets	⊘○○○○
___ station (five-letter min.)	○○○○
Four Beatles	○○○○
Four four-letter colors	○○○○
Gear for a goalie or catcher	○

41

"Make a difference, even
in the smallest way."

—*Kate Middleton*

journaling prompts

Sit quietly for a few minutes, breathing and listening to your body before you begin.

What past challenge has turned out to be a gift in disguise (even if it's still painful)? Why? Reflect on the silver lining.

· ·

If I knew that anything I asked for would be answered, I would ask for _____.

· ·

What is a new skill that I would like to learn and how can I learn it?

· ·

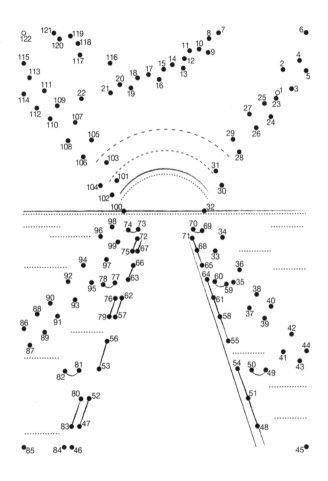

44

"Hopeful thinking can get you out of your fear zone and into your appreciation zone."

—*Martha Beck*

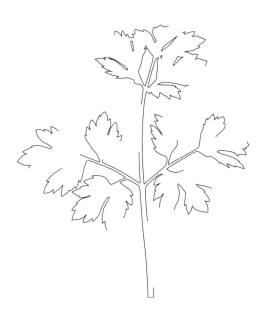

49

SPA DAY By Anna Gundlach

ACROSS

1. Music players at raves or weddings
4. Bow of silent movies
9. Rock's ___ Speedwagon
10. Thingamabob
11. ". . . and so forth"
12. Relaxing spa day activity
13. How pie might be served
15. Prescription, briefly
16. Relaxing spa day activity
18. End-of-the-week exclamation
19. Put the first chips in the pot
23. Relaxing spa day activity
27. French friend
30. High-end German sports car brand
31. Relaxing spa day activity
33. Belonging to that guy
34. Grippers in a toolbox
35. Crystal ball, e.g.
36. Adjusted to, as a thermostat
37. Digs for pigs

DOWN

1. Had night visions?
2. International traveller's woe
3. "You know who else is able to do that? Me!"
4. Like a secret message
5. Easy toss
6. Man in first place?
7. Freelancer's fee
8. Condition treated with Ritalin, for short
10. "Whoa, bro"
12. Deck-swabbing tool
14. Rub the wrong way
17. Food with a paw print logo
20. Cheese-covered bar food
21. Top bought at a concert, maybe
22. Just barely gets through
24. No longer united
25. Teeth on a wheel
26. Before, poetically
27. Roadies' hauls
28. One way for someone to present their gender identity
29. "That so?"
32. Mermaid's home

"One of the best ways to hold
onto your happiness is simply
by saying, 'Thanks.'"

—*Jennifer Dukes Lee*

```
D C O R O L L A N H C M
E U Z Y N Y Y N E Y G A
S V C X E V R E G D C R
O A A K K V U P O R A S
O C R N C E C T R O M U
G U G E I N R U T G R I
T U O O H U E N I E Y R
C M N N C S M E N N Z P
```

find and circle

Four types of poultry	⦻○○○
Four gases	○○○○
Four planets	○○○○
Three Toyota models	○○○
Outer space, e.g.	○

nature's music meditation

Find a spot outside where you can sit or stand
comfortably. Take a few moments to focus on your
breathing. Gradually begin to bring your awareness
to the sounds of nature surrounding you. Is there
birdsong, wind in the trees, or insects singing?
Try to focus on these sounds. If your mind wanders,
don't get frustrated or judge yourself, calmly bring
your attention back to the sounds of nature.

```
L L X J P N V Z J E E P
J I Z L O U R A X G P Z
X O M M I E L Z N N O A
P N E E T Z W P P A L M
U L J S B Z A E X R P A
M X B R H U E R S O X L
P O A Z J P S Z D T Z L
L C T A N G E R I N E X
```

find and circle

Four citrus fruits	⊘○○○
Four animals with names that begin with "L"	○○○○
Four words that begin and end with "P"	○○○○
Four types of automobiles	○○○○
The ____ Indies	○

"Happiness is not something ready made. It comes from your own actions."

—*Dalai Lama*

Tea By Anna Gundlach

ACROSS

1. Fruit-filled dessert
4. Weightlifting units
8. 24-hr. cash source
9. South American cornmeal cake
11. Herb sometimes used for its calming properties
14. One way to talk online
15. Clean, like one's brow or hard drive
17. Herb sometimes used for its calming properties
20. Alphabetically-first Jackson 5 single
23. Channel for vintage films
24. Lamb's mom
25. Herb sometimes used for its calming properties
28. Three of a kind
29. Garden entrances
33. Herb sometimes used for its calming properties
36. Bring out a meal
37. Caustic chemical used in making bagels
38. They change regular eggs to Easter eggs
39. Brewpub fixture

DOWN

1. Lacking color
2. Shopping list line
3. Jane Austen heroine
4. Didn't finish on time
5. Unit of work
6. RPM part
7. Reproduce, like salmon
10. Tangential remark
12. First thing in the pan, in many recipes
13. Gush out
16. Sonneteer's "before"
18. Pre-DVD device
19. People seeking polictal asylum
20. ABA member
21. Dinner table faux pas
22. Shows sadness
26. Motorcycle's small cousin
27. Zoom need, for short
30. Pinball error
31. "Orinoco Flow" singer
32. Part of a dance move
34. Snoop
35. The day before a holiday

"The power of finding beauty in the humblest things makes home happy and life lovely."

—*Louisa May Alcott*

```
G  G  Z  F  L  A  S  H  X  E  K  C
A  O  X  D  J  G  E  H  F  Z  N  E
L  R  A  X  E  L  O  F  A  O  B  T
L  D  Z  T  L  C  A  P  B  I  E  U
I  O  R  E  S  R  A  B  H  B  L  N
R  N  Z  A  I  N  I  D  I  E  Z  I
O  A  V  G  I  G  O  T  E  X  R  M
G  S  E  C  O  N  D  W  J  G  N  U
```

find and circle

Seven mammals starting with "G"	⊘○○○○○○
Three six-letter units of time	○○○
Three four-letter forms of precipitation	○○○
Comic strip that debuted in 1934: ____ ____	○○
Himalayan region	○

65

"Ask questions. Sniff around. Remain open. Trust in the miraculous truth that new and marvelous ideas are looking for human collaborators every single day."

—*Elizabeth Gilbert*

T I R O N G F R E N C H
Z H R X I Z R S X H X H
A Z A U J T E E S J S N
R P B I S N A I E I G A
A U A D A S N L L K O M
B M T P O A I G I Z L R
I A A K P V N A X A D E
C J Z S Z E E Z N J N G

find and circle

Ten languages	⊘○○○○○○○○○
Two four-letter metals	○○
Shoe brand or type of cat	○
Bird that rhymes with "love"	○
It's used in cricket or baseball	○

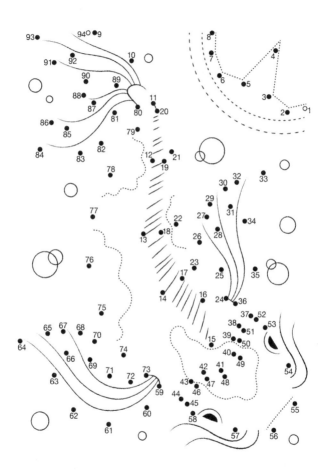

find and circle

Eight words related to poker	⊘OOOOOOO
Three human joints	OOO
Two Canadian cities	OO
Frosty the ____	O
Star Wars character played by Ford	O

journal prompt

Sit quietly for a few minutes, breathing and listening to your body before you begin.

Who do I most admire? Why?

. . . .

If I could ask my future self one question, what would I ask and why?

. . . .

If I could relive one moment, what would it be?

. . . .

"Ultimately, happiness is really just about enjoying life."

—*Tony Hsieh*

```
M P H A R E S M I L E N
W U U G R I M A C E N I
L O L M P L U M H E Y R
F I L E A X T C D A K G
P R O F Z S A E W R R X
X E O N E E W R I E N Z
C G A W P S O M E Y J B
B O A R N N S D L C G C
```

find and circle

Eight four-letter mammals	⦾○○○○○○○
Five facial expressions	○○○○○
Three fruits starting with "P"	○○○
Two Scandinavian countries	○○
Direction of the sunset	○

"It is a fine seasoning for joy
to think of those we love."

—*Molière*

Tranquility By Anna Gundlach

ACROSS

1. Special attention, for short
4. Jaden Smith, to Will
7. Make forbidden
10. Sigh of satisfaction
11. Chaperones
13. State of calm and ease
15. "Farewell, mon ami!"
16. Welcome at the front door
17. 3-Down, for example
19. Govt. broadcasting overseer
20. State of calm and ease
24. Issa of "Insecure"
25. Stereotypical cowboy's nickname
26. Partner of "each"
29. Socially forbidden thing
33. State of calm and ease
35. Large supply of something, metaphorically
36. Play a part
37. "Gangnam Style" rapper
38. That woman
39. Prefix meaning "new"

DOWN

1. "Later!"
2. Ingredient in pie crusts or refried beans, sometimes
3. Spiced beverage from India
4. Video game with a number in the title, often
5. Buckeye State coll.
6. CBS crime series
7. Alternative to boxers
8. Places to store holiday decorations when not in use
9. "Bye Bye Bye" boy band
12. Cheer for a bullfighter
14. ___ pot (nosecleaning device)
18. PC key under X
20. Relishes each bite
21. Itsy-bitsy
22. Stinging plant
23. Optometrist's checkup
24. Postgame summary
27. Google Maps abbr.
28. Urges
30. Lima or pinto
31. Just this time
32. Bart's bus driver
34. Slangy refusal

"Happy are those who dare
courageously to defend what
they love."

—*Ovid*

find and circle

Eight European capitals	⊘○○○○○○○
Four rodents	○○○○
Two four-letter metals	○○
Lake Mead creator: _____ Dam	○
Penny or nickel, for example	○

81

visualizing breath

Take a few deep breaths. In through your nose, out through your mouth, paying attention to the sensations of your breathing.

. . . .

Try to visualize the inhaled breath as a color. Picture a path the color follows as it goes in through your nose and fills up your lungs.

. . . .

Now, try to visualize your exhaled breath as a different color. As the air circulates in your lungs, imagine that it changes color and creates a path back out through your mouth.

. . . .

Repeat for several breath sequences.

. . . .

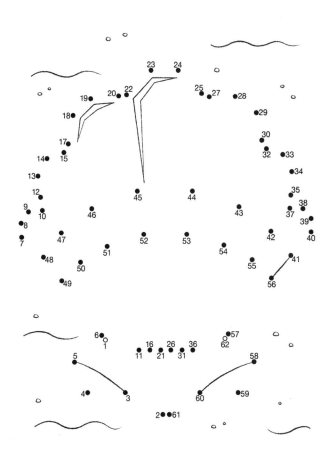

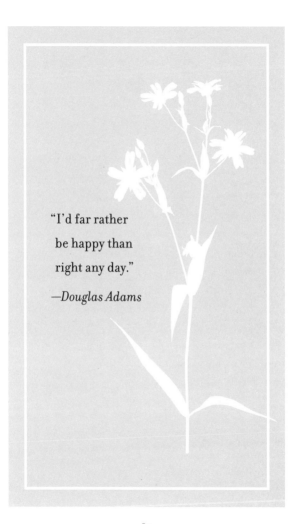

"I'd far rather
be happy than
right any day."

—*Douglas Adams*

cat and cow stretch

These yoga stretches can help release tension in your lower back.

To begin, kneel on all fours with your hands shoulder-width apart and your knees right below your hips.

. . . .

As you breathe in, arch your back, and draw your belly toward your spine while dropping your head as you tuck your chin into your chest.

. . . .

As you breathe out, reverse the movement by lifting your tailbone upward and tilting your head and chin back.

. . . .

Repeat this for at least five breath cycles.

. . . .

YOGA By Anna Gundlach

ACROSS

1. Hooded serpent
6. Pirate ship feature
11. Month when many Aries are born
12. Be a snitch
13. Clothes lines?
14. Yemeni's neighbor
15. Traveler's respite
16. Make all payments on
18. Part of a web address
19. Quaint word on a shoppe sign
21. "Oh, give ___ rest"
23. Positions of tranquility, as seen in the asnwers to the starred clues
27. United
28. Purple stonefruit
30. Rage
33. Bouncers check them
35. "Who wants pie?" response
36. Wi-Fi connection need
38. Disney theme park in Orlando
40. Big name in home appliances
41. Interchangeable
42. Caravan mount
43. Flower related to the water lily

DOWN

1. Japanese maker of watches and keyboards
2. In an unashamedly candid way
3. "A Streetcar Named Desire" star
4. Edge of a goblet
5. To boot
6. Lickety-split
7. Hasty escape
8. Hardly any at all
9. Off-limits act, to a child
10. Make mittens, say
17. Cleaned, like a windshield
20. Narcissist's trait
22. Venomous serpent
24. "The Muppets" drummer
25. Bring forth, as a response
26. Puzzle with many numbers but no arithmetic
29. Tiny flecks
30. All-in-one Apple
31. Oblong tomato
32. Yellow dutch cheese
34. Wax emblem on an envelope
37. 67.5 degrees on a compass
39. Mahmoud Abbas's grp.

"Blessed are they who see beautiful
things in humble places where
other people see nothing."

—*Camille Pissarro*

```
R A R M Y A T H E N S S
S O H I T C H S P P B A
N B M S Y X S A X U N P
I U V E N R Z Z C N X A
L L Y M A R I N E S Y R
R L X E Z X Z I P X V I
E S B D C C V A L I A S
B Z O O W A R S A W N B
```

find and circle

Six European capitals	⊘○○○○○
Four words that start with "Z"	○○○○
Three branches of the U.S. military	○○○
Three Chicago sports teams	○○○
Two Will Smith movies	○○

"Success is liking yourself,
liking what you do, and liking
how you do it."

—*Maya Angelou*

```
F  F  C  A  R  J  F  F  C  T  E  N
T  I  R  Z  C  C  E  A  I  Z  X  B
W  V  V  O  J  O  A  E  L  F  K  A
E  Y  Z  E  G  X  N  N  P  C  T  Y
N  T  U  R  K  E  Y  D  A  K  O  Y
T  P  A  R  R  O  T  X  O  R  Z  N
Y  H  H  E  A  R  S  E  Z  R  Y  C
T  R  U  C  K  O  N  E  V  A  N  G
```

find and circle

Five common denominations of U.S. currency	⊘ ○ ○ ○ ○
Five six-letter birds	○ ○ ○ ○ ○
Five motor vehicles	○ ○ ○ ○ ○
Four-letter amphibian	○
Three-letter body of water	○

95

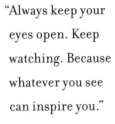

"Always keep your eyes open. Keep watching. Because whatever you see can inspire you."

—*Grace Coddington*

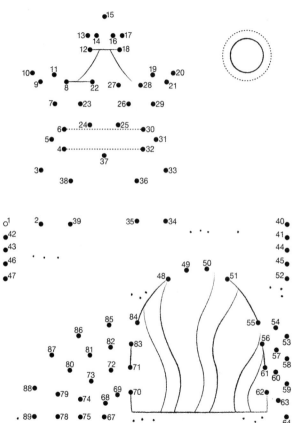

gratitude

Write down five things in your life that you're grateful for. Consider making gratitude practice a part of your routine. Get a gratitude journal and try to jot down a few things you're thankful for at the end of each day. The list can be short or long, simple or as detailed as you want. Practicing mindful gratitude can help train your mind to look for the positive no matter what life throws your way.

"Happiness is when what you think, what you say, and what you do are in harmony."

—*Mahatma Gandhi*

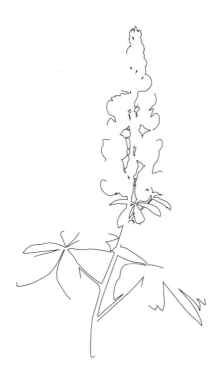

ZZZ'S By Anna Gundlach

ACROSS

1. Massively popular K-pop septet
4. Thanked the audience
9. Rowdy hooligan
11. Place for outpatient health care
13. Russian monarch all suited up for a joust?
15. "Hungry Hungry" board game animal
16. Video chat alternative to Zoom
17. Cute ___ button
19. Talk like a kitten
20. Affliction that causes foggy vision and smoky thoughts?
24. Word on a gift tag
25. Uno y due
26. Take ___ (get some shut-eye)
29. At just the right moment
33. Get some shut-eye, like the answers to 13- and 20-Across?
35. Sounds from a cave
36. Taking care of the situation
37. Scarfed down
38. Airport screening agy.

DOWN

1. Uninspired
2. "Cornflake Girl" singer Amos
3. Kind of rhyming pump
4. Letters representing pre-AD years
5. Auto company founded in 1897
6. Lit part of an oil lamp
7. Digestive protein
8. New parent's purchase
10. November birthstone
12. Ocean liner's staff
14. Like an optimistic outlook
18. Rear, on an ocean liner
20. Ancient poet who coined "carpe diem"
21. Franklin who was the first female performer in the Rock and Roll Hall of Fame
22. Suffix with switch or buck
23. Mobile payment app owned by PayPal
24. Confront head-on
27. Citizen of Glasgow
28. You, archaically
30. Fifth of a nickel
31. '80s action movie weapons
32. This, in Spain
34. Nine-digit ID no.

"Never dull
your shine for
somebody else."

—*Tyra Banks*

"All of the qualities—yes, even the flaws—that make you, YOU, also make you interesting, capable, and powerful in your own way. You just need to own them."

—*Sarah Knight*

notes

....

....

....

....

....

....

....

....

....

....

....

....

notes

solutions

SOLUTIONS

ATHENS, LISBON,
BERLIN, MADRID,
WARSAW, VIENNA,
ROME—TROUT, PERCH,
SHARK, SMELT—
CONFLICT, LOLLIPOP—
CHEF—MILE

3   word roundup

5   dot to dot

10   spot the differences

12   crossword

114

RAPTOR, RADAR,
RIDER, RIVER, RULER,
RAZOR, RUMOR,
REAR, ROAR—GOBLET,
STEIN, CUP, MUG—
EXCHANGEABLE—
VENUS—GUAVA

15   word roundup

DROOL, FOOL, COOL,
TOOL, OOPS, WOOL—
SALSA, SAMBA, WALTZ,
TANGO, MAMBO,
SWING—OFFENSE,
DEFENSE—EXCEL,
WORD—CUP, MUG

18   word roundup

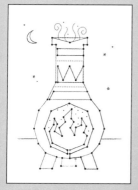

19   dot to dot

24   spot the differences

SOLUTIONS

		I	D	O		P	L	A	N
	S	P	A	M		R	O	M	E
	T	I	A	R	A		E	X	P	O
D	O	E	S	T	H	I	S		
E	R	R			A	L	T	O	I	D
M	A	R	I	E		K	O	N	D	O
S	H	A	M	M	Y			A	I	R
			S	P	A	R	K	J	O	Y
T	O	F	U		R	A	N	A	T	
O	D	O	R		D	R	E	G		
E	D	G	E			S	E	W		

26 crossword

ALGERIA, JAMAICA,
SOMALIA, TUNISIA,
RUSSIA, CANADA,
PANAMA, CHINA,
LIBYA, CUBA—CREAM,
MILK—FRUIT—
COIN—OWL

29 word roundup

31 dot to dot

36 spot the differences

	G	I	V	E			I	Z	O	D
H	O	T	E	L		A	S	I	D	E
I	S	A	A	K		R	A	N	I	N
R	O	L	L	S	R	O	Y	C	E	
E	L	I			A	A	S			
R	O	C	K	I	N	R	O	B	I	N
			E	N	D			A	B	E
	R	A	V	E	R	E	V	I	E	W
A	I	S	L	E		S	I	T	A	T
S	T	E	A	D		S	E	E	M	S
H	E	A	R			O	D	D	S	

38 crossword

HAMSTER, FISH, BIRD,
DOG, CAT—TELEVISION,
SUBWAY, TRAIN,
RADIO—GEORGE,
RINGO, JOHN, PAUL—
PINK, GRAY, BLUE,
TEAL—MASK

41 word roundup

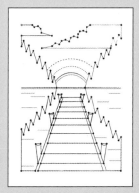

44 dot to dot

48 spot the differences

117

D	J	S			C	L	A	R	A
R	E	O		D	O	O	D	A	D
E	T	C	M	U	D	B	A	T	H
A	L	A	M	O	D	E		M	E	D
M	A	N	I	P	E	D	I		
T	G	I	F			A	N	T	E
		F	A	C	E	M	A	S	K
A	M	I		P	O	R	S	C	H	E
M	A	S	S	A	G	E		H	I	S
P	L	I	E	R	S		O	R	B
S	E	T	A	T			S	T	Y

50 crossword

CHICKEN, TURKEY,
GOOSE, DUCK—
NITROGEN, HYDROGEN,
ARGON, NEON—
NEPTUNE, MERCURY,
VENUS, MARS—COROLLA,
PRIUS, CAMRY—VACUUM

53 word roundup

55 dot to dot

TANGERINE, ORANGE,
LEMON, LIME—
LOBSTER, LIZARD,
LLAMA, LION—PULP,
PUMP, PLOP, PEEP—
JEEP, CAR, BUS,
VAN—WEST

57 word roundup

60 spot the differences

62 crossword

| GIRAFFE, GORILLA, |
| GAZELLE, GIBBON, |
| GOPHER, GOAT, GNU— |
| SECOND, MINUTE, |
| DECADE—RAIN, |
| SNOW, HAIL—FLASH, |
| GORDON—TIBET |

65 word roundup

| JAPANESE, ITALIAN, |
| SPANISH, ENGLISH, |
| RUSSIAN, GERMAN, |
| ARABIC, FRENCH, |
| GREEK, THAI—IRON, |
| GOLD—PUMA— |
| DOVE—BAT |

67 word roundup

69   dot to dot

STRAIGHT, FLUSH,
RAISE, FOLD, PAIR,
HAND, ANTE, BET—
KNUCKLE, ANKLE,
ELBOW—MONTREAL,
TORONTO—
SNOWMAN—SOLO

70   word roundup

MULE, PUMA, WOLF,
LION, LYNX, HARE,
DEER, BOAR—GRIMACE,
SMIRK, SMILE, FROWN,
GRIN—PEACH, PEAR,
PLUM—NORWAY,
SWEDEN—WEST

74   word roundup

76   spot the differences

T	L	C		S	O	N		B	A	N	
A	A	H		E	S	C	O	R	T	S	
T	R	A	N	Q	U	I	L	I	T	Y	
A	D	I	E	U		S	E	E	I	N	
			T	E	A		F	C	C		
	S	T	I	L	L	N	E	S	S		
R	A	E			T	E	X				
E	V	E	R	Y		T	A	B	O	O	
C	O	N	T	E	N	T	M	E	N	T	
A	R	S	E	N	A	L		A	C	T	
P	S	Y		S	H	E		N	E	O	

78   crossword

ATHENS, BERLIN,
WARSAW, LISBON,
MADRID, VIENNA,
PARIS, ROME—HAMSTER,
BEAVER, MOUSE,
RAT—IRON, GOLD—
HOOVER—COIN

81   word roundup

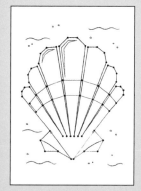

83   dot to dot

88   spot the differences

121

C	O	B	R	A		P	L	A	N	K
A	P	R	I	L		R	A	T	O	N
S	E	A	M	S		O	M	A	N	I
I	N	N		O	W	N		D	O	T
O	L	D	E		I	T	A			
	Y	O	G	A	P	O	S	E	S	
		O	N	E		P	L	U	M	
I	R	E		I	D	S		I	D	O
M	O	D	E	M		E	P	C	O	T
A	M	A	N	A		A	L	I	K	E
C	A	M	E	L		L	O	T	U	S

90 crossword

ATHENS, BERLIN,
WARSAW, VIENNA,
PARIS, ROME—ZANY,
ZOO, ZIP, ZAP—
MARINES, ARMY,
NAVY—BEARS, BULLS,
CUBS—HITCH, ALI

93 word roundup

ONE, FIVE, TEN,
TWENTY, FIFTY—
TURKEY, CONDOR,
PARROT, FALCON,
CANARY—HEARSE,
TRUCK, JEEP, CAR,
VAN—FROG—BAY

95 word roundup

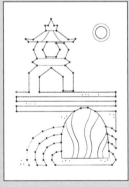

97 dot to dot

122

102 spot the differences

104 crossword

108 spot the differences

Andrews McMeel Publishing
a division of Andrews McMeel Universal
1130 Walnut Street, Kansas City, Missouri 64106

www.andrewsmcmeel.com

20 21 22 23 24 RLP 10 9 8 7 6 5 4 3 2 1

ISBN: 978-1-5248-6697-6

Editor: Allison Adler
Art Director: Julie Barnes
Production Editor: Jasmine Lim
Production Manager: Tamara Haus

ATTENTION: SCHOOLS AND BUSINESSES
Andrews McMeel books are available at quantity
discounts with bulk purchase for educational,
business, or sales promotional use. For information,
please e-mail the Andrews McMeel Publishing
Special Sales Department: specialsales@amuniversal.com.